W9-AMV-120

ELVIS IS EVERYWHERE

PHOTOGRAPHS BY ROWLAND SCHERMAN

EDITED BY

MARK POLLARD

Clarkson Potter/Publishers, New York

ELVIS USED THIS FITTING PLATFORM
MANY TIMES IN HIS CAREER.

HE STOOD TALL AND PROUD HERE,
AS HE STANDS IN OUR MEMORY.

July 22nd/95

Dear Mom,
   Happy Birthday!
Hope you enjoy the book!
       Love,
       Dallas

Elvis is Everywhere

This book is dedicated to Molly Reily, my best friend.
-Rowland

Copyright © 1991 by Second Son Publications.
Photographs copyright © 1991 by Rowland Scherman.

All rights reserved. No part of this book may be reproduced or
transmitted in any form or by any means, electronic or mechanical,
including photocopying, recording, or by any information storage
and retrieval system, without the permission in writing from the publisher.

Published by Clarkson N. Potter, Inc., 201 East 50th Street, New York, New York 10022.
Member of the Crown Publishing Group.

CLARKSON N. POTTER, POTTER, and colophon are trademarks of Clarkson N. Potter, Inc.

Design by Mark Pollard and Paul Pollard for Second Son Publications, New York.

Manufactured in the United States of America.

Library of Congress Cataloging-in-Publication Data

  Scherman, Rowland.
    Elvis is everywhere/photographs by Rowland Scherman; edited by
  Mark Pollard. — 1st ed.
        p.   cm.
      1. Presley, Elvis, 1935–1977—Pictorial works.   I. Pollard, Mark.
  II. Title.
  ML88.P76S33   1991   91–3409
  779' .9782166—dc20   CIP
                                              MN
ISBN 0-517-58605-3

10 9 8 7 6 5 4 3 2 1

First Edition

Introduction

About three years ago, I went looking for Elvis. Actually, it might be more accurate to say that he came looking for me. I first noticed him turning up in my photographs on a roll of film I shot in New York City in May 1989. Unseen until the film was processed, there he was in the background — a face on a T-shirt smiling down on a kissing couple, a name on a passing bus, a reflection in a shop window.

I became fascinated by this discovery. Just how pervasive was this phenomenon, I wondered. Was it just this roll of film? Just this street? Still musing, I walked into a New York bookstore to discover, in the philosophy section, a bit of memorable graffiti. Some wag had edited (read: defaced) a RETURN BOOKS TO SHELVES sign to read TURN TO ELVIS. I got the message. Elvis, it seemed, was everywhere.

From that day on, I never had far to look for signs that Elvis's presence is palpably among us. In the past year I've visited Boston, Los Angeles, Nashville, Venice Beach, Orlando, Nag's Head, Cape Cod, New York, Pasadena, and, of course, Memphis, gathering evidence that Elvis lives, at least in spirit, long after his well-mourned death. In Chicago friends showed me a rock-oriented McDonald's where Elvis dominated the decor, inside and out, and a bar that displayed the tabloid news that Elvis's statue had been discovered on Mars. In the French Quarter in New Orleans I nearly stumbled over a horse whose name was Elvis — that's what it said on his hat, anyway.

And what have I learned from my visual pilgrimage? That this book is not so much about Elvis as it is about *us*. The abiding loyalty and reverence of the King's devoted fans have enabled him to transcend even the most outrageous promotional hype. His image and his name have been absorbed into the language, the landscape, our very culture. Elvis continues to cast his spell on our collective consciousness, and I do not see any end to it.

What I did see is here, in these photographs.

—Rowland Scherman

6

ICKET INFORMATION/SALES WINDOWS

Special "Elvis" film at Graceland Plaza.
Tours depart from the loading area to your left.
Your tour number is on your ticket and will be called in order.
ADULTS $7.50 **CHILDREN** $4.75
SENIOR CITIZENS $6.75
65 & OLDER I.D. REQUIRED

ELVIS' AIRPLANES
A short introductory film-tour Elvis' Jetstar "Hound dog II".
Then tour the flying Million dollar apartment-the Lisa Marie.
Tours begin in theatre through gift shop to your Left.
ADULTS $3.95 **CHILDREN** $2.75
SENIOR CITIZENS $3.50
65 & OLDER I.D. REQUIRED

ELVIS' RECREATIONAL BUS
Tours run continually.
ADULTS & CHILDREN $1.00

"ELVIS - UP CLOSE"
Exhibit at Graceland Plaza.
A Rare Glimpse At The "Personal" Elvis
ADULTS & CHILDREN $1.75

"IF I CAN DREAM"
Special film at Graceland Plaza begins every 30 minutes
ADULTS & CHILDREN $1.50

THE ELVIS PRESLEY AUTOMOBILE MUSEUM
A display of Elvis' cars,
motorcycles, toys and more
ADULTS $3.50
CHILDREN $2.50

COMBO TICKET PACKAGE #1
INCLUDES ALL ATTRACTIONS
ADULTS $16.95 **CHILDREN** $10.95
SENIOR CITIZENS $14.35
65 & OLDER I.D. REQUIRED

COMBO TICKET PACKAGE #2
Graceland Mansion Tour
"If I Can Dream" Film
Elvis' Airplanes
The Elvis Presley Automobile Museum
ADULTS $14.95 **CHILDREN** $9.95
SENIOR CITIZENS $13.45
65 & OLDER I.D. REQUIRED

COMBO TICKET PACKAGE #3
Graceland Mansion
"Elvis-Up Close" Museum
"If I Can Dream" Film
The Elvis Presley Automobile Museum
ADULTS $12.95 CHILDREN
SENIOR CITIZENS

COMBO TICKET PACKAGE
Elvis' Bus and Airplanes
"Elvis-Up Close" Museum
"If I Can Dream" Film
The Elvis Presley Auto
ADULTS $9.95 **CHILDREN** $6.95
SENIOR CITIZENS $8.95
65 & OLDER I.D. REQUIRED

OPERATION SCHEDULE

- Graceland tours are available
seven days a week. March - October
Mansion closed Tuesdays, November-
February 28. Other attractions
are available at this time. Closed
Thanksgiving Day, Christmas Day
and New Year's Day

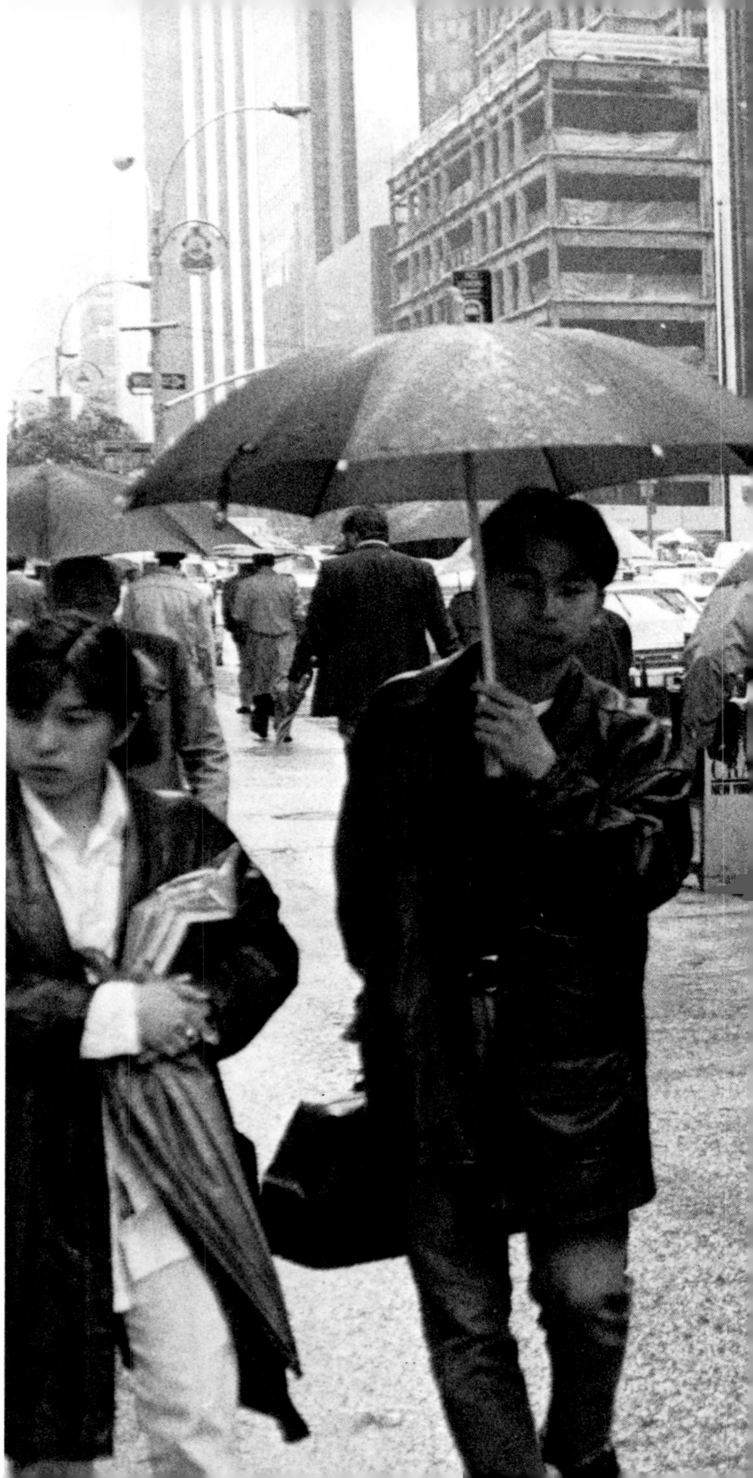

50,000,000 ELVIS FANS
CAN'T BE WRONG

List of Plates

About the Photographer

Rowland Scherman began taking pictures in New York in 1958. In 1961, he served as the first photographer for the Peace Corps. Scherman has done covers and photojournalism for *Life, Time, Newsweek, Paris Match, Playboy,* and *National Geographic.* He won a Grammy in 1968 for an album cover for Bob Dylan, and in 1969 was voted Photographer of the Year by the Washington Art Directors' Association. He lived in Britain for seven years, and there created the book *Love Letters,* also taking time to herd sheep and work as a carpenter in South Wales. Scherman now lives in Birmingham, Alabama, where his work includes landscape photography and portraiture.